THE NINTH CIRCLE

Olexa Woropay

The Ninth Circle
In Commemoration of the
Victims of the Famine of 1933

Edited with an Introduction by
James E. Mace

To Al
With best regards
and fond memories of
Ann Arbor
J.E. Mace

Harvard University
Ukrainian Studies Fund
Cambridge, Massachusetts

The Ukrainian Studies Fund, Inc. was established in 1957. Its purpose is to raise funds for the establishment and support of Ukrainian scholarly centers at American universities. The organization has endowed three chairs in Ukrainian studies (history, literature, and linguistics) at Harvard University, and is in the process of completing the endowment of Harvard's Ukrainian Research Institute.

Contents

Photo Insert

Photos following page 8 were first published in *The Chicago American* newspaper during February and March, 1935.

Editor's Introduction

James E. Mace

READERS IN THE English-speaking world will find much of what Olexa Woropay says hard to believe. The world he describes with such eloquent simplicity is completely alien to anything they have ever experienced: it is cut from the same cloth as Hitler's death camps, a world gone mad on the blood of human beings sacrificed on the altar of political expediency.

When Americans think of the Soviet Union, they tend to think of Russia and assume that all those who live there are Russians. In fact, about half the inhabitants of the USSR are not Russian at all; they belong to nations as diverse as Armenians in the South, Lithuanians in the North, Muslim Kazakhs and Tatars, and an array of Siberian peoples not unlike our own American Indians. There are over one hundred languages spoken in the Soviet Union, and Russian is only one of them.

According to the 1979 census, over forty million of the Soviet Union's inhabitants were Ukrainians, a Slavic nation like the Russians and Poles as different from them as they are from each other. The Ukrainians have a historical record that extends back to the tenth century when their ruler, Prince (St.) Volodymyr accepted Christianity and brought what was then called Rus' into the ranks of the Christian nations of Europe. They have a rich culture of which they are rightly proud, and the central figure of their literary tradition is the poet Taras Shevchenko, a nineteenth-century bard who was born a serf and rose to the highest levels of cultured society in the Russian Empire. The reader will learn from Woropay what happened in Shevchenko's native village in 1933.

In 1933 Ukraine and certain neighboring areas were victims of what those who survived remember as the *Velyky Holod*, the Great Famine or, more precisely, the Great Hunger. It is also often referred to as *Shtuchny Holod*, the Artificial or Man-Made Hunger, for it was not, like most

ix

famines, due to some natural calamity or crop failure. Figures on the Ukrainian harvest were published in the press at the time, and they show that the grain crop was only a little below the pre-collectivization average; there was certainly no crop failure capable of causing a famine. A few years earlier the Soviet government had collectivized agriculture, forced the farmers to give up their individual farms, pool whatever resources could be taken from them, work the land in common on estates not unlike that on which Shevchenko worked as a serf, and give a far greater share of what they produced to the state.[1] The farmers fought against this, and they also fought for their national culture, which was under attack by the Soviet regime. It was in order to break this resistance that government agents were sent into the countryside and ordered to take away all food stuffs. As a result, the people starved.

We have far more than Woropay's word for this. For one thing, we have census figures published by the Soviet government, and we have various other official Soviet population studies, which allow us to put the census figures in perspective. According to Soviet Ukrainian figures from the late twenties and early thirties, the number of Ukrainians in the USSR was increasing at well over one percent a year.[2] Yet, the 1939 census — itself somewhat suspect[3] — shows that the number of Ukrainians declined by almost ten percent, over three million people, from what it had been in 1926 when the last published census was taken.[4] A

---

[1] Khrushchev admitted the following in a speech delivered before the Supreme Soviet of the USSR in 1958: ". . . what did collective farm property consist of in, say, 1929–30? It was simply the socialization of village property — horses, plows, *sokhas* (a type of wooden implement which merely scratches rather than turns the soil), harrows, and some outbuildings." M. S. Khrushchev, *Pro dalnyi rozvytok kolhospnoho ladu i reorhanizatsiiu mashynno-traktornykh stantsii* (Kiev: 1958), p. 35. For a comparison of the harvests of the early thirties, lower than before collectivization, with the much higher levels of what was taken from the farmers, see Naum Jasny, *The Socialized Agriculture of the USSR: Plans and Performance* (Stanford: 1949), pp. 61–102.

[2] V. I. Naulko, *Etnichnyi sklad naselennia Ukrains'koi RSR: Statystyko-kartohrafichne doslidzhennia* (Kiev: 1965), p. 84.

[3] A similar census was done in 1937, but it was withdrawn before distribution and everyone who conducted it was shot, probably because it showed too clearly the population losses brought about by the famine. Boris Souvarine, *Stalin: A Critical Survey of Bolshevism* (New York: 1939), p. 669.

[4] V. I. Kozlov, *Natsionalnosti SSSR: Etnodemograficheskii obzor* (Moscow: 1975), p. 249.

Polish Communist historian calculated from these figures that there were 9.3 million fewer Ukrainians in 1939 than would have been expected from the population trends of the 1920s.[5] Some of this was due to a lowered birth rate during the famine and some to assimilation at a time when Soviet government was actually attempting to destroy Ukrainian culture, but this still leaves several millions who could only have perished from starvation and famine-related diseases.

There are also thousands of eye-witness accounts like those Woropay presents. The Harvard University Refuge Interview Project conducted interviews with thousands of displaced persons who left the Soviet Union during and shortly after World War II, and the project files contain hundreds of accounts virtually identical with those in this book. Many more survivors published accounts of their experiences in books of testimonies published by Ukrainian groups in the West. They have highly emotional titles like *The Black Deeds of the Kremlin* and *Moscow's Biggest Crime*. After one reads Woropay's book, one might begin to understand how these people became so emotionally and vehemently anti-Communist. For Ukrainians, Communism has come to be just another name for Russian imperialism, one even more oppressive than the tsarist imperialism under which their grandparents lived. There are also quite a number of Western accounts by non-Ukrainians.[6]

Lastly, we have one truly unimpeachable source. Nikita Khrushchev, who ruled the Soviet Union from the mid-fifties until 1964, related the following in his unofficial memoirs, published in the West from tape recordings smuggled out of the USSR after his death:

> Mikoyan told me that Comrade Demchenko, who was then First Secretary of the Kiev Regional Committee, once came to see him in Moscow. Here's what Demchenko said: "Anastas Ivanovich, does Comrade Stalin — for that matter, does anyone in the Politbureau — know what's happening in the Ukraine? Well, if not, I'll give you some idea. A train recently pulled into Kiev loaded with corpses of people who had starved to death. It had picked up corpses all the way from Poltava to Kiev . . ."[7]

---

[5] Janusz Radziejowski, "Collectivization in Ukraine in Light of Soviet Historiography," *Journal of Ukrainian Studies*, No. 9 (1980), p. 17.

[6] For a survey of predominantly Western sources, see Dana Dalrymple, "The Soviet Famine of 1932–34," *Soviet Studies*, XV: 3 (January 1964), pp. 250–284; XVI: 4 (April 1965), pp. 471–474.

[7] N. S. Khrushchev, *Khrushchev Remembers* (Boston and Toronto: 1970), p. 74.

The fact that Khrushchev was not in Ukraine at the time and can only give the story second-hand does little to undermine its credibility. Khrushchev might have lied about many things, but he had no reason to lie about this.

In order to understand why the famine of 1933 occurred, one must go back at least to 1917, perhaps even to 1900 when the first Ukrainian political parties were formed in the Russian Empire. The Ukrainians were at that time almost entirely a nation of peasants, just as the Czechs had been not long before. If one visited Prague in, say, 1800, the language one would hear in the streets and shops would have been German, not Czech. Only later was Prague "Czechized." By the same token, the cities of Ukraine were predominantly Russian-speaking in 1917. Although they were largely Ukrainized in the late 1920s, they were later re-Russified to the point where today Ukrainian is seldom heard in the streets of Kiev. In order to prevent the development of a Ukrainian national movement, the tsarist Russian government made it illegal to write or publish in the Ukrainian language up to 1905. The concessions made in that year were gradually withdrawn to the point that very little could be published legally in Ukrainian by the time the First World War broke out. Ukrainian writers had two choices: either publish legally in Russian and hope to slip something past the censor through the use of Aesopian language, or publish in Ukrainian in Austrian-ruled Western Ukraine (Eastern Galicia) and try to have their work smuggled over the border illegally. Despite these obstacles, the Ukrainians produced an educated stratum, the intelligentsia, and this group organized political parties, which sought national liberation, social justice for the peasants, and some sort of home rule for Ukraine.

In 1917 the Russian Empire disintegrated. The tsar abdicated, the police were slaughtered or went into hiding, and the imperial army began to fall apart. The Russian Provisional Government had little real power, particularly in outlying areas. A Ukrainian national council, the Central Rada, was organized in Kiev. Led by the two largest Ukrainian socialist parties, the Socialist Revolutionaries and Social Democrats, it gradually evolved into an autonomous national government. After the Bolsheviks took power in Petrograd and began an invasion of Ukraine, the Rada declared Ukraine independent in January 1918. For years, Ukraine was fought over by Ukrainian governments, the Bolsheviks, Denikin's Russian Volunteer Army (which sought to turn the clock back to before the revolution), the Poles, and a number of rural warlords known as *otamans*. Although by 1921 the Bolsheviks were able to defeat their various rivals in the field of battle, large-scale guerrilla warfare continued in the Ukrainian countryside. Ukrainian governments were driven from the country, but the Ukrainian peasantry remained unconquered.

The Bolsheviks decided to concede the peasants the minimum of what they demanded. In 1921 the New Economic Policy was adopted, ending forced requisitions of foodstuffs and allowing farmers to sell their products in a limited free market. In 1923, a series of policies known as indigenization were adopted in non-Russian areas. These policies provided for the recruitment of non-Russians into the Party and state, teaching Russians the local language, and actively supporting the cultural life of the non-Russian poples. Belorussianization, Tatarization, Yiddishization, and so forth, proceeded through the rest of the decade.

Since the Ukrainians of all the non-Russian nations were the most numerous and constituted the greatest political threat to Moscow, Ukrainization went much farther than any of its counterparts. Many prominent Ukrainian intellectual and political leaders returned from exile to take advantage of the cultural opportunities afforded by this relatively benevolent policy. A national cultural revival of unprecedented creativity took place in literature, scholarship, and the arts. Even within the Communist Party (bolshevik) of Ukraine, a strong Ukrainian wing demanded that Ukrainization lead to the end of Russian domination. This group, led by Oleksander Shumsky, Mykola Khvyl'ovy, and Mykhailo Volobuev, was condemned as "nationalistic deviationist," and the Party repudiated their views.

By the end of 1927 Mykola Skrypnyk emerged as Ukraine's political strongman. His official post, Commissar of Education, placed him in charge of the Ukrainization policy and of supervising cultural life in general. By eschewing any hint of anti-Russian sentiment, he was briefly able to achieve much of what Shumsky, Khvyl'ovy, and Volobuev had called for. Under Skrypnyk, Soviet Ukraine evolved more and more in the direction of a national government, defending its prerogatives from Moscow and even demanding it be allowed to defend the national interests of Ukrainians residing in Russia itself.

The regime used the respite provided by the New Economic Policy and Ukrainization to penetrate the Ukrainian countryside in a variety of ways. Committees of Non-Rich Peasants (*komnezams*, KNS), which had earlier seized peasants crops and held absolute power in the villages, were retained. There was no counterpart to these organizations in Russia. After 1925 they were stripped of political power and turned into voluntary organizations, and during collectivization and the early stages of the famine they played an important role in expropriating those the regime wanted to get rid of, forcing the peasants into collective farms (*kolhosps*), and searching for hidden grain to seize. In this later period, however, they often performed these functions under the leadership of someone sent from the outside to supervise dekulakization, collectivization, and the deliveries of grain to the state. Village soviets were also organized, and the countryside was covered by a dense network of secret police collaborators known as the *seksoty*. Because of this penetration of the countryside, the regime was in a far stronger position relative to the peasants than it had been in 1921. Whereas the Bolsheviks had hitherto come to the villages as complete strangers, they now had organized supporters ready to do their bidding and provide information on potential opponents who could be singled out for elimination.

Stalin saw the nationalities question and peasant question as indissolubly linked. In his view, the peasants constituted the social basis of national movements, the reservoir from which such movements drew strength. As he once put it, "The nationality problem is *by its essence* a peasant problem."[8] Thus, concessions to the peasants meant concessions to the non-Russian nations and vice versa. By the same token, repression in the countryside and repression against those nations were bound to go together. They were two sides of the same coin.

In 1929 Stalin decided to eliminate the kulaks (well-to-do peasants, *kurkuls* in Ukrainian) as a class, begin forcing peasants into collective farms, and use what could be taken from the peasants to finance rapid industrialization. This was possible because, although collectivization did nothing to increase crop yields (the current problems of Soviet agriculture are largely attributable to forced collectivization), harvesting was done in common, and the state could supervise the harvest directly and take as much as it wished directly from the threshing room floor. This is precisely what happened, and the idea that the state should take all it required from "first proceeds," that is, the threshing room, became known as the First Commandment of Soviet agriculture.

At the same time as peasants were being forced into collective farms the first steps were taken to end the indigenization policies. Since Ukraine was the largest stumbling block, these steps took the form of indirect attacks on Skrypnyk and his clients. In 1929 one of his most

---

[8] I. V. Stalin, *Sochinennia* (Moscow: 1946–1951), VII, p. 72.

important subordinates, the ideological watchdog of historians, Matvyi Yavorsky, was attacked for "treating the history of Ukraine as a distinctive process."[9] The political implication of such a charge was quite obvious: if Ukraine did not have its own history, it was not a distinctive country and ought not to be considered as such. This was the beginning of the end of Skrypnyk. At the same time, the Ukrainian Autocephalous Orthodox Church was banned and its priests were executed on a mass scale. In 1930 a show trial was held of an imaginary conspiracy called the Union for the Liberation of Ukraine. At this trial some of Ukraine's most distinguished intellectual and spiritual leaders were convicted of a host of crimes known in the jargon of the day as "wrecking." Among these charges was a most interesting one: linguistic sabotage, which consisted of spelling words in such a way as to make the Ukrainian language closer to Polish than to Russian. Despite the absurdity of this charge, it held particularly ominous political implications for Skrypnyk, who had participated directly in various linguistic discussions of the 1920s. When Skrypnyk was denounced and removed from his post in 1933, one of the major charges levelled against him was that he had advocated the use of the letter G in Ukrainian.[10]

The famine of 1933 succeeded in breaking the Ukrainian peasantry as a political force, completed the destruction of the entire social structure of the Ukrainian nation, and made possible far-reaching political changes. In addition to the fall of Skrypnyk, the Ukrainization policy was ended and a policy of Russification was instituted. The Ukrainian wing of the Communist Party ceased to be an independent policy force and over the next several years what was left of its old cadres were "liquidated" (a singularly inappropriate euphemism since such people did not melt; they were executed), and the Ukrainian intelligentsia was to all intents and purposes destroyed. Ukrainian culture was thus decapitated by the loss of its intellectual and political leaders, pushed out of the cities and back on the farms by a return to Russification, and Soviet spokesmen began to glorify everything Russian, including the tsarist past. At roughly the same time, internal passports were issued to urban dwellers but not to collective farmers. Since farmers could not live in the cities and towns without such documents, this meant legally attaching the agricultural population to the land. The word customarily used to describe such a state of affairs is serfdom.

---

[9] *Istorik-marksist*, XII (1929), p. 285.
[10] *Visti VUTsVK*, June 22, 1933 and June 30, 1933.

Author's Introduction

WE BOW OUR heads before the graves of millions of victims whom Communist Moscow caused to die the grimmest of deaths — the death of starvation — in the year 1933 in Ukraine.

To understand the tragedy fully, one must remember that this wholesale murder of peasant farmers took place in one of the richest countries of world, with its fertile 'black soil'. People died of starvation in a country which abounded in harvests, sufficient not only to feed her own population, but also to rank her among the leaders in the world export market of good hard wheat. In the famine year the victims perished in what has been rightly called the "grain-store" of Europe. The bolsheviks themselves call it the "bread-basket of the U.S.S.R."

The enemy occupying Ukraine, red Moscow, organized this infamous famine in order to bring defiant Ukraine to her knees by means of this punishment, unheard-of in its cruelty, and thus to make of her an obedient colony.

In 1929 there started what the communists used to call "complete collectivization, based on the liquidation of 'kurkuls' as a class." 'Kurkuls' — kulaks in Russia — were better-off peasant farmers, tilling their own soil, but employing labor outside their immediate family. In the plain language of the people, collectivization thus meant that the communists intended a general and thorough plunder of the peasants. The peasants of Ukraine, foreseeing a new form of slavery, protested openly. In 1930–31 many peasant risings occurred in Russian-occupied Ukraine, but these were ruthlessly quelled by the communist regime. The following are a few examples of what occurred.

xvi

In June 1931, a cavalry regiment was sent from Proskuriv to suppress a riot of peasants in the village of Mykhailivka, in the Dunaivtsi district of Kamianets-Podillia province. The military operation was directed by the commanding officer of an army corps, a certain Diomin. He ordered the surrounding of the village on every side and its destruction and burning by artillery fire. After the village had gone up in flames, the whole male population — from fifteen years upwards — was arrested by the security forces. Over three hundred men and over fifty women were deported from the village on that occasion by the Stalin "heroes." Not a single one of those deported ever returned to this village. Such was the punishment for resisting collectivization, though this process was at one time actually proclaimed to be a voluntary movement.

In September 1930, there was a riot in the village of Rudkivtsi in Podillia. The peasants rioted, protesting against the collective farms — called 'kolhosps'*. When land surveyors arrived to mark off the land for a kolhosp, peasants expelled them. Two days later, they returned to the village with police protection, but the police were also driven away by the villagers. After another three days, a detachment of security police came from Vinnytsia with full battle equipment. These armed "heroes" surrounded the village and forced it to surrender. They then entered it, and picked out twenty-eight people from among the most active rioters. Two of them — Ivan Haiduchenko and Ostap Prokhnytsky — were shot on the spot, without any sort of trial, while the others were deported, and their further fate is not known to anyone . . .

In 1929 and 1930, in the neighborhood of Bila Tserkva, near Kiev, a detachment of insurgents were operating under the leadership of "Otaman" Shpak, a veteran hero of the Ukrainian struggle for liberation in 1918–19. The word shpak is also a bird's name. Such terror was spelled by it to the Russian communists that even yet peasants make jokes about the way it was forbidden to call the bird by its proper name at the time of collectivization.

"Call it 'skvorets'," they used to say, "because 'shpak' means counter-revolution."

A group of peasants commanded by Vrublevsky were also fighting in the Kiev region. Vrublevsky himself was a former Petliurist, but the majority of his comrades-in-arms had been 'red partisans', who had at last realised the true nature of their partisanship.

---

* In Russia 'kolkhozes.'

Many popular risings in the Kuban and Don areas were widely known about at that time, and were cruelly suppressed by the Russians.

Moscow understood that all this marked the beginning of a new Ukrainian war, and she was afraid, remembering the liberation struggle of 1918–21. She knew, too, how great a threat an economically independent Ukraine would be to communism — especially as there still remained in the Ukrainian villages a considerable element which was both nationally conscious and morally strong enough to cherish the idea of an independent, unified Ukraine.

Thus, in order to enslave and finally to subdue the people of Ukraine, it was necessary to attack and to weaken her in some way. The communists feared an open struggle because of the hostility of the masses. Red Moscow therefore adopted a most ignominious plan to break the power of resistance of the thirty-five million strong Ukrainian nation. The strength of Ukraine was to be undermined by famine.

During the preparation of that unheard-of crime, as earlier during collectivization and the liquidation of the kurkuls, Moscow sought the support of the local Russian Communists, of criminals, and of other morally debased elements.

In 1932, soon after the harvest, detailed plans for the requisition of every kind of crop were imposed on the Ukrainian peasants. But Ukraine, ruined as she already was by collectivization and the liquidation of kurkuls, could meet neither the grain quotas nor any other economic plans. The misery and shortages already beginning in Ukraine did not, however, trouble Moscow at all.

Under direct pressure from Moscow, the Council of People's Commissars of the Ukrainian S.S.R. resolved on December 6, 1932, as follows:

1. Immediately to stop supplies to certain localities, and interrupt all government and commercial activity there. To close the governmental and co-operative shops, and to withdraw all merchandise from them.

2. To forbid trading in essential consumer goods, which was then being carried on by kolhosps and individual farmers.

3. To refuse any credit to the population of those localities and to call in credits which had already been issued.

4. To review the personnel of the administrative and economic organizations and to remove hostile elements from among them.

5. To act similarly throughout the kolhosps, removing from them counter-revolutionary elements who engage in sabotage.

The paper *Proletarska Pravda* on December 10, 1932, commented favorably on this "historical" decision of the Council of People's Commissars of the Ukrainian S.S.R. and spoke of the Ukrainian peasants as "the traitors of the interests of the proletariat."

In brief, the government was not governing, but was virtually in a state of war against its own people.

On January 11, 1933, at the combined plenary session of the Central Committee and the Central Control Commission of the Communist Party of the Soviet Union* Stalin delivered a speech about party work among the peasants — "on our work in the country". Stalin emphasised that the chief fault of the party's activities in the country were the difficulties attached to the carrying out of grain delivery plans: primarily in Ukraine, where " . . . in charge of the kolhosps are former followers of Petliura, who have devised new tactics of 'soft undermining'."

After Stalin's speech, the Central Committee and the Central Control Commission of the C.P.S.U.,in their resolution of January 24, 1933, stated that the Central Committee of the Communist Party of Ukraine had administered the grain deliveries in Ukraine most unsatisfactorily. Its management of kolhosps was also far from satisfactory, and it had further shown a "lack of class vigilance". This latter was apparently most evident in the so-called "key provinces of Ukraine", those of Kharkiv, Dnipropetrovsk, and Odessa. In order to remedy this state of affairs, and to "help" Ukraine, the Central Committee of the C.P.S.U. sent Pavel P. Postyshev to take over the post of Secretary to the C.C. of the C.P.(B) of Ukraine, and also of the first secretary of the Kharkiv Provincial Executive Committee, and of the local Executive Committee.

Similarly, the posts of the secretaries of the provincial Executive Committees of Dnipropetrovsk and Odessa provinces were taken over by Khataevich and Veger, both sent from Moscow. Besides those three "aces," ten thousand "experienced and proven" Communists sent from Moscow and Leningrad, the so-called "ten-thousanders." All these were put into key posts in the district and village councils, the kolhosps and so on. they became chairmen and treasurers of the kolhosps, secretaries of the district party committees, and chairment of the district executive committees — that is, of the administrative committees.

---

* Hereafter C.P.S.U.

But that was not the end of it. Together with Postyshev, Khatayevich and Veger, Balytsky, the former chief of the local G.P.U., arrived in Ukraine to take over the post of chief of security police. Nor did he arrive alone: "experienced and proven" men accompanied him, too. Two years earlier, Balytsky had performed the functions of Menzhinsky's deputy in Moscow; now he was returning to Ukraine with a "good" training.

And still there was more to come.

For in concluding his speech Stalin had said: " . . . I think that the political departments of the M.T.S. (Machine Tractor Stations) are one of those means which will assist in decisively eliminating these shortcomings at the earliest possible date." And accordingly, the political departments of the M.T.S. and "sovkhozes" — state farms — were dispatched from Moscow and Leningrad to Ukraine. There were six hundred of such "political departments" sent, and each consisted of five people: a chairman and four deputies, including one in charge of security matters and another in charge of "Komsomol" — the Union of Communist Youth. This number did not include attendants, the majority of whom were imported from Muscovy, because the local population was not be trusted. Many brought their families with them too . . .

This whole monstrous horde of Russian Communists, like a pack of beasts of prey, threw itself on an already impoverished and plundered Ukraine. Contacts were quickly made with the Russian bureaucracy which had earlier been set up, which had by this time acquired considerable experience in the "art" of despoiling the peasants, and which had also organized around them sinister and criminal elements from among the local "Komsomol" members. These latter, along with other party activists, armed themselves with long iron rods, sharpened at one end, and commenced their deadly work.

In every village, all over Ukraine, day by day, hour by hour, these mobs visited one house after another in search of grain. They pierced floors with their iron pikes, probed the walls, dug holes in the farmyards, orchards, vegetable gardens, and roamed across the fields and meadows.

They took away everything edible they could find: grain, flour, pearlbarley, and so on, leaving entire families without a piece of bread.

"What shall I feed my children with?" cried out a window in the village of Kurylivka, near Khmil'nyk in Podillia.

"Pust' dokhnut vmeste s toboi!" (in Russian: let them croak with you!) replied the deputy chief of the "Politotdel" (political department) of the Uladiv M.T.S., a young Russian from Leningrad — the "city of Lenin."

The peasants managed to survive in great privation until the spring. But in that spring their bodies began to swell and they began to die of hunger. A horror was commencing which is justly known as the madness of the devil in our pious Ukraine.

THE NINTH CIRCLE

CHAPTER ONE

What I Saw With my Own Eyes

1. The Villages in My Sector

1.

IN THE SPRING of 1933 I was working as an agronomist in a sector of the Uladiv M.T.S. (Machine and Tractor Station) near Vinnytsia. My sector extended along the river Bug, six miles away from Khmil'nyk, a typical small provincial town in Podillia.

The villages I served were essentially Podillian, with rich apple orchards and vegetable gardens, reaching down to the river bank, and with green meadows spreading in a long belt along the quietly-flowing Bug.

I was living in the village of Klityshcha, which was about the largest and most prosperous village in my sector. In the farmyards there still remained some of the earlier farm buildings: barns, store-rooms, stables, pigsties. In the orchards kilns for drying cherries and apples might yet be seen. The houses, too, were not completely stripped of thatch and whitewash, as they were in some other villages. All these were signs of former prosperity. With some reason, then, the Russian Communists called Klityshcha a 'kurkul village.'

On every possible occasion the peasants recalled those more fortunate times when they themselves were masters on their own farms. They had not always been well-off, but at least they had not had to deal with the kolhosps, or with the 'authorized agents' who swarmed like locusts into the villages.

Besides apple orchards and luxurious vegetable gardens this particular village preserved a tradition of horse-breeding.

"There was a time," the peasants would say, "when we used to go to

1

the fair at Khmil'nyk; no-one troubled to ask whose horses we brought — he had only to glance at them and he knew instantly they were from Klityshcha!''

But all this was many years ago. Now, one could hardly see a resemblance to horses in the objects which stood in a long, semi-dark stable, under a roof of reeds. They looked more like shabby, distorted scarecrows, chewing dry chaff cut from last year's straw.

Horses fared badly in the kolhosp, but people fared even worse. I remember the first time I saw a human being with a body swollen from starvation, just out there in the kolhosp yard by the stable. He was an old, grey-haired man who came to work in the kolhosp with an axe. Under his eyes were two pocket-like swellings, and the skin on them had a peculiar glassy tint. His hands were swollen, too. On his fingers the swellings had burst, and the wounds exuded a transparent liquid with an extremely repulsive smell.

Later on in the same spring, and in that same village of Kiltyshcha, I had many miserable opportunities of seeing far more horrible scenes of human suffering, but this — the first case — made the greatest impression on me. Even now, twenty years later, after experiencing and witnessing so much distress, I cannot rid myself of the sight of that earlier tragedy.

I was then a young man of twenty, looking out on the world through rose-colored spectacles — as the saying goes — and I was then ignorant of the fact that behind the cleverly-woven camouflage of bolshevist propaganda those very scenes — the scenes of starving people — were the most real things of all.

This was in April, and, as yet, a man with his body swollen from hunger was an unusual sight.

May brought rainfall: it rained nearly every day, and all green things grew buoyantly. In uncultivated gardens, orchards, by the roadside, wherever there was an inch of soil, enormous weeds grew. Starving people rushed at the verdure and started to eat cooked orrach, sorrel, nettle — anything which could possibly seem edible to a starving human body.

But after consuming such wild plants — and often eating them raw — people suffered from dropsy and died from starvation in great numbers. In the second half of May, the death rate from starvation was so great that a kolhosp wagon was specially set aside for the purpose of carrying the dead each day to the cemetery.

These bodies were thrown down, several into one grave, and covered with earth without any customary or religious rites. The debasement of human dignity was carried to the limit.

And Stalin, in a speech of January 11, 1933, said: " . . . We have the power, we dispose of the resources of the state, we are called upon to manage the kolhosps, and it is we who should bear all responsibility for the work in the country . . . " (Report in *Pravda*, January 17, 1933.).

We and our descendents will hold the Bolsheviks to that responsibility in full.

2.

The chief of the political department of the M.T.S. in Uladiv was a sailor from Kronstadt. Drunken and cruel, he would shout at the meetings of the workers and staff of the M.T.S.: "Take away the grain up to the last kernel! Snatch away the material basis of the counter-revolution! Force the peasants by hunger to work in the kolhosp! For these are the directives of the Party and of the Government."

The work of the kolhosps did not prosper. Sugar beet plantations were overgrown with weeds, the sowing of cereals was delayed until the end of May, while in the kolhosp orchards and gardens the wolves howled. Everything in short, lacked proper care.

The "Kronstadt sailor" used to go to and from the kolhosps in his shining car, and, not understanding anything about agriculture and ignoring the sufferings of the peasants from hunger, he saw all shortcomings as evidence of 'soft undermining' by kurkuls and Petliurists.*

A typical remark of his was: "To be deprived of his job and handed over for trial for sabotage and the disruption of the kolhosp." And on the next day, the security deputy of the chief of the political department would appear to take the matter over formally, while on the third day the victim would disappear .

Thus in the course of one spring dozens of chairmen of kolhosps, foremen of workers 'brigades,' and field overseers vanished.

The deputy in charge of Komsomol was a young student who had not finished his education and came from Leningrad. He used to ride in a carriage and pair, with a coachman to drive him — not in a car, as his boss did.

On one occasion in May he arrived at the sugar beet plantation of the

---

* Petliura was the head of the Ukrainian Directory in its struggle for independence, 1981–1921.

Klityshcha kolhosp. I happened to be on the plantation just then and was busy preparing a solution of Barium Chloride to sprinkle the beets against caterpillars.

"Chto eto ty delaesh?" (in Russian: *What* are you doing?) asked the deputy.

I explained.

"And has this poison any effect on man?" he demanded.

"Yes, it has. It causes the drainage of water from the tissues, so that paralysis results. Death is slow and painful."

At my reply, he beckoned me away: "Come, sit down here in my carriage. We'll go to the village."

I sat down as bidden, and we departed. On the way he told me that sombody had stolen some preserved apples from his landlady's cellar, and he liked these apples so much! It was true that not all were taken, one barrel still remained intact. Now he wanted to trap thief, and it occurred to him he might make a solution of Barium Chloride, put some apples into it, and then leave the door open . . .

"Let him gobble till he's satisfied," he chuckled, "Eh? Ha, ha. He'll have a little pain in his stomach — eh?"

I said I had run short of Barium Chloride, that I had used all I had on the beet — and incidentally, that it would not be a humane thing to do . . .

"Ha-ha-ha! Humane!" his voice rasped. "Humanism is a petty-bourgeois theory. We, brother, construct socialism with firm hands. No use here for baby tears."

I tried to move him. "So many people die from hunger nowadays, their bodies swollen. For instance, yesterday . . . "

But he would not listen. "Don't talk, enough of it, I say. They are all enemies of the Soviet rule, those who die. It's a trifle, we've got plenty of peonle."

And then he shouted to the driver: "Grisha, go faster. I am hungry."

3.

It was a beautiful sunny day. The apple orchards were in full bloom, bees were humming, from time to time a swallow flew above one's head or a sparrow fluttered up. A peaceful and happy scene.

I was driving along the main street of Kurylivka village. The horse plodded on slowly, and I did not hurry up. There was nothing to hurry for, and around me was a sea of apple blossoms — wonderful!

But neither in the street nor in the farmyards did I see anybody. And this was typical of that period. People rarely appeared in the street. Those who were fit enough went to work in the kolhosps, because barley groats were cooked there and one was given one meal of it a day. Those who were already too weak to walk stayed at home or sat somewhere in the woods and were scarcely ever seen by the casual eye.

When I approached the school I saw a boy of about ten years of age sitting in the sun, with bowed head, as if he were slumbering. I recognized him as Mykola, who often used to unharness my horse on the kolhosp farmyard.

I halted and shouted to him. "Mykola, come here, have a drive with me!"

The boy raised his head weakly, looked at me indifferently and bent down again. I left my cart, came up to him and asked:

"What's wrong with you, Mykola? Are you ill?"

He replied simply: "I am hungry!"

I had a piece of bread with me, and took it out of my briefcase and gave it to him. Mykola took the bread an began to gnaw . . .

When I returned that way in the evening, on my way home, I saw Mykola lying dead. In his hand was a piece of bread which he had not finished eating.

4.

A friend of mine, Borys Oleksandrovych, was the doctor in the village of Klityshcha. Like me, he had only recently finished his studies and was starting his career by working as the local physician. Jokingly he called himself the "sectoral enema-syringe." So many people so often had intestinal trouble that the syringe was very fashionable. Borys Oleksandrovych throughout the whole spring did not part for an hour from his special bag in which reposed a glass bottle with a long rubber tube and peculiar end-piece.

Naturally, we often talked together about current events. I learned from him that according to a special secret order of the "appropriate authorities" all deaths from hunger had to be registered as cases of infectious disease.

At the end of May, when the death-rate reached its climax, the Bolsheviks came to their senses. Following an order of the district council of the "People's Health Commissariat," Borys Oleksandrovych set up "nutrition centers" in the villages of his sector.

Once I went with him to see a "center." It was the one in our village of Klityshcha. It consisted of two empty peasant houses which stood side-by-side. In both of them there were slanting wooden platforms instead of beds, covered with straw. On them men, women, and children lay together. Somebody had written one night on the door: "Thanks to Comrade Stalin for our Happy Childhood."

The doctor was assisted by two young women who fed the "infected" milk and a thick buckwheat porridge. The great majority did not survive. Women and girls seemed to exist more easily than men and boys. If out of ten males six happened to survive, Borys Oleksandrovych called it "good fortune."

The bodies of the dead were removed to a cool cellar, where they usually lay until the evening. Then a kolhosp wagon would drive up, collect the corpses, and carry them to the cemetery.

While I was watching there, a woman and two children — a mother with her two sons, one six years old, the other eight — were carried away into the cellar. Their father, still a young man, was lying just beside them and looked on while the bodies of his wife and two children were removed. He did not weep, no tears flowed from his eyes, but his look was one that I shall never forget as long as I live.

Later I asked about this man, and was told that he had survived. He had, however, left the village. I wonder whether he lived to take part in the fighting of the last war, and to go into the battle for "The Motherland! For Stalin!"

5.

One day Borys Oleksandrovych joined me on my "bidarka" (cart) and we started off for a neighboring village. The weather was warm and fine. In the fields by the road enormous wild flowers were growing with blossoms of many colors. Red poppies abounded among the clumps of white, blue, and yellow blossoms.

Suddenly we heard something stir among the flowers. There was a kind of mewing, like that of a kitten. We halted, climbed down and began to search among the weeds. We did not have far to look before we found a young woman in an embroidered blouse, with a white scarf on her head, bare-footed, laying there newly dead. Her blouse was opened, and on her nude, exhausted breasts crawled and cried a hungry baby. At her side lay a white scarf folded carefully. Opening it, we found a passport. The woman was twenty-two, and had come from the village of Kozhukhi, which was about thirteen miles away from Klityshcha.

We took the baby — a little girl — with us, and Borys Oleksandrovych handed her over to the nutrition centre.

She remained alive. I wonder whether anyone ever told her what became of her mother . . .

6.

A Machine and Tractor Station is a state-owned agricultural base with tactors, mechanics, agronomists, and its own N.K.V.D. — political department, that is, secret police, the successor to the G.P.U., and now known as K.G.B.

Nominally an M.T.S. had its own manager, but in reality, in 1933, everything at the station was subordinated to the political department in the person of its chief.

We, the sector agronomists, had to forward each week to the political department a written account of our own work and that of the kolhosp. This consisted of economic information: how much land had been ploughed, sown, cleared of weeds, and so on. The reports were sent by messenger, not by post, as the mails took too long.

One day a friend of mine, Panas Tymofievych, the agronomists of a neighbouring sector, sent his report as usual by messenger. This time the messenger was a man aged about forty, but so weakened by starvation that he was not able to work in the fields.

He had a long way to go, more than six miles, He was not given a horse, so he went on foot. He did not arrive at the M.T.S., but died on the way.

The political department did not receive the required information. The next day the 'Kronstadt sailor' summoned Tymofievych by telegram to come and see him in his office. When my friend arrived, the chief beat the table with his fists and shouted:

"Why didn't you send your report at the proper time?"

"I did send one, Comrade Superintendant," my friend replied, "but the messenger died on his way here."

"What do you mean, died? Why send a sick messenger." demanded the chief.

Tymofievych explained: "There are no fit ones, Comrade Superintendant, the whole village is starving. Those who are most fit work in the fields, and a weaker one was sent . . . "

"Want does this mean 'is starving'? There is no starvation in the Soviet Union. Now remember — you are listening to kurkul rumors." And after this outburst, he bent his head over the table, hiding his eyes like a thief. In a softer way he added:

"Get out. And, look here, mind you keep your mouth shut."

7.

Work in the kolhosps did not, as I have remarked already, proceed very successfully. The greatest difficulty was with the sugar beet. In the second half of May the beet needed hoeing, work that is very laborious and impossible to mechanise.

Women of the kolhosp, exhausted as they were by hunger, could not manage the job properly. A 'brigade' of women — twenty-five to thirty of them — would start out on the rows of beets, but before they came to the other end of a field, half of them had fallen out and were having to lie and rest where they were, among the rows of beets.

One day the chief of the political department passed by along the road and, seeing women resting in the field, decided to discipline the chairman of the kolhosp for 'such a mess.' He went to the village, found the chairman in his office and went for him.

"What a muddle! The hags should work properly — Soviet industry is waiting for raw materials, and they — just look at them — are lying comfortably about on the plantation, like idle ladies!"

The chairman of the kolhosp, a local peasant, explained to him as clearly as he could that the women were not 'lying comfortably,' but that they were unable to keep on working owing to lack of strength.

The chief was not satisfied. "That's a lie, you pawn of a kurkul! I will go myself to the field! I will have to talk with them, if you, nincompoop, cannot manage them."

And so he went. It was 'dinner-time.' As everywhere else, the workers were cooking a meal out in the field on the sugar beet plantation — a meal of pearl-barley or oat groats. As the best field was bounded at one end by a wood, many women took groats in their dishes to eat in the coolness among the bushes. At that moment a car drew up, and the chief of the "politotdyel" climbed out of it.

Without waiting to greet anyone, he began to shout:

"What are you sitting so nicely among the bushes for? Just look at these fine ladies! Soviet industry . . . "

"And you, son-of-a-bitch," shouted several voices, "can't you see that our legs are swollen from hunger? Eh?

The chief of the political department, *persona grata*, was not prepared for such a counter-attack. As he turned round to see who dared to reply to him in such a way, another woman — plopped a dish of groats on his head.

At this signal the women swooped like crows on the 'sailor' from all

DELIBERATE STARVATION OF PEASANTS

A typical Ukrainian peasant jailed for two years, returned to his starving village.

This corpse is that of the father of the boy pictured at the right. The orphaned child was unable even to bury his parent. There were no shovels in the village since the last raid of the OGPU, and the boy could only cover the body with straw. (All photos copyright, 1935, by American Newspapers, Inc.)

Villages Depopulated by Hunger in Ukraine as Soviet Punish Their Opponents

STARVATION stalks through the Ukraine section of Soviet Russia, leaving a ghastly trail of death and agony. The Ukraine is the most fertile grain producing district in Russia.

The facts contained in the series of articles, of which this is the first, were obtained by Thomas Walker, an

American newspaper man, now resident in London, at the peril of his life. When Mr. Walker entered Russia last Spring he smuggled in a camera.

While photographs shown with these articles were obtained under the most adverse and dangerous possible circumstances, the evidence they present is more grim and graphic than words.

BY THOMAS WALKER,

Noted Journalist, Traveler and Student of Russian Affairs, Who Has Spent Several Years Touring the Union of Soviet Russia.

This fifteen year old son of the peasant at center, could only cover his father's body with straw.

Corpses remained unburied after the political police seized all shovels in the village.

Peasant women garnered grain spilled in sowing.

Horses died of starvation, their masters unable to beg fodder.

Death at the side of the road.

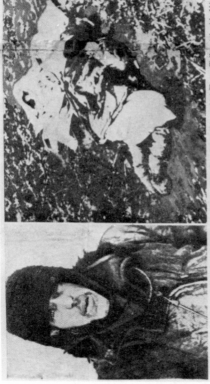

A "dekurkulized" peasant who escaped from Siberia and returned to find his wife and child gone.

As the mother died by the roadside, her baby crawled only inches before it perished also.

"I want to die and be with my mother," cried this homeless orphan girl, found wandering on the

Father in a concentration camp, mother gone two days in search of food, this boy must wander alone,

This homeless Ukraine boy, ill with fever, carried water in a bucket to quench his incessant thirst.

Death from starvation in a Soviet hay cart! Weary from
to keep life in his body. Weary from
forced labor, he crawled into this hay ca
to find rest. His eyes closed—and ne
opened again.
Although he worked on a communally farm where food was plentiful, this peasant could not get enough to eat.

(All Pictures Copyright, 1935, by American Newspapers, Inc.)

A starving peasant who died in a haycart.

In his article describing the enforced
fa**e in the Ukraine, Thomas Walker
t**'s of finding this little Russian peasant
bo**s reading beside his dying father and
we**ing bitterly. The father had been
shot for approaching too closely to forbidden territory while the two were picking up grains of wheat spilled on the ground. Now the boy must wander alone, almost certainly to die of starvation.

A peasant boy cried as his father lay dying; shot while picking up
grains spilled on the ground.

Homeless children (bezprizorni) who wandered the country seeking food.

sides at once. They poured hot soup over him, and he was soaked from head to foot.

There was among the others one woman — Andrii's wife Kalyna — who was one of those Ukrainian women of whom it is said that 'the earth burns under her.' Kalyna grasped a large ladle used for stirring, rushed at the 'boss,' and began to cross examine him:

"And you, devil's trap, where's our wheat? Where's our bacon? Can we weed the beet, if we eat only groats?"

And the big ladle swept across his back, once, twice, again . . . When the 'sailor' realized his was no mere joke, he jumped into his car, and made off.

Next day everyone expected the police to arrive. Kalyna took a bag with her and hid in the woods. But nothing happened. Not on the next day, nor the one after, did anyone arrive . . .

The chief of the political department, no doubt, felt ashamed of being 'bathed with groats' by women. Apparently, he did not tell anyone of it, neither the police nor even his wife.

II. A Trip to Kiev

1.

IN THE BEGINNING of June, I was summoned by the chief agronomist of the M.T.S., who suggested to me that I should go to Kiev to attend a special course of instruction at the People's Commissariat for Agriculture of the Ukrainian S.S.R., dealing with the treatment of crops for insect pests. I agreed and received a travel warrant, some pocket money, and set off.

While living at the village I had no idea of conditions on the railways. I found those conditions comparable to the biblical account of the building of the tower of Babel.

Between Vinnytsia and Kiev all stations, big and small, were glutted with people, littered with coats, high boots, bare feet, white scarves, corsets, embroidered blouses, and — always — sacks, sacks and sacks. Sacks were on everybody's shoulders, on those of women, men, girls, and children alike.

When the train halted, such crowds collected at every door such that,

even if the cars had been ten times their size, they would not have been
big enough to accommodate everyone. People climbed on to the roofs,
broke through windows, quarrelled with the militia, with the railways
officials, and with each other . . .

"Where are we going to, auntie?" one would say.

"Eh, son, better not to ask. Would I drag my old bones along with a
sack on my back if it were not for the children? I don't pity myself, but
the children . . . "

In a third class compartment, packed with people, I somehow found
myself in a seat by the window. Opposite me was a young man, a crafty-
looking type, perhaps a kolhosp book-keeper. He was learning over his
bundle and dozing. I noticed he was trying not to fall asleep, and thought
he was perhaps afraid of being robbed. Cautiously I spoke to him in a
whisper:

"Do you come from far off? I think I've seen you somewhere before.
Perhaps you are going to Kiev, and, in that case, we might as well travel
together."

"I am from Kalynivka," he replied, "and am going rather a long
way. I've tried Kiev already, but there's the police . . . it's not much
use there."

I asked again: "Perhaps to Moscow this time . . . ?"

Now he spoke more readily. "They don't let you go there. I would
like to go — there's plenty of bread, I know. One of our people was
there — everything is cheap and plentiful. I'm going to Kursk — it's not
so expensive there, either."

And he went on to tell me that he had already been beyond Kursk, and
had bought one 'pood'* and a half of rye flour, taken it home, and was
now on his way for more food, since what he had brought would not last
until the next harvest. There was no hunger in the town he had visited,
there were ample stocks of food and it was only the numbers of our own
hungry people who had caused flour and potato prices to rise there.
Earlier, everything had been cheaper, but now thirty-five or forty rubles
was demanded for one pood of rye flour. Potatoes had been three rubles
a 'mera,'** but now cost seven.

I asked him how much these things cost in our own market.

"In ours it's very expensive. Flour is 250–500, potatoes 85–90

---

* A pood is equal almost to 73 pounds.
** A mera roughly equals 44 pounds.

rubles a pood. And, what is worse, one cannot buy these things except on the 'black market.' It's forbidden to trade, so that the militia would confiscate the goods, if they found out.''

"But in Russia," I inquired, "is it not also forbidden?"

"No, there it is not. You may trade there as much as you wish. The markets are like they were here during the N.E.P."*

Overhearing our talk about bread and markets, the man sitting beside me joined in our conversation, and later on a harsh bass voice from the upper deck intervened. Little by little, hesitantly, the whole wagon started to chatter.

From that chatter and from the stories told then I learned that a great number of people were travelling to Russia for bread. It was forbidden to go there, and the railway booking offices did not issue tickets to those who had no warrant. People tried extraordinary tricks, used fictitious stories, merely to travel to that hated Muscovy, to purchase a little of something edible in exchange for the last fur-coats, for carpets, and linen, to bring it home and so to save their children from dying of hunger.

Somehow they succeeded in getting through to Russia, but to return — that was a much more difficult task. One was not allowed to enter passenger cars with luggage, and so it was necessary to slip on to freight trains.

By day and night, from Russia into Ukraine there were empty trains being sent to the elevators and enormous granaries of the Zahotzerno — the Soviet state organization for the buying up of grain — which were overflowing with Ukrainian grain.

People would climb in stealthily with their baggage and travel in the empty freight cars, risking at every moment the loss of their precious cargo they hoped would save the lives of families impatiently waiting for them at home.

Transport security police used to raid the trains. N.K.V.D. men dealt ruthlessly with the ''sack-carriers,'' confiscating the baggage and money, often sending those caught to prison, or deporting them to those special camps from which no-one ever returns alive.

The railway personnel robbed the peasants, too. Engine drivers con-

---

* N.E.P. was the New Economic Policy, a more liberal approach to the economic problems of ownership put into action by Lenin in 1921, after the failure of so-called ''War Communism.''

spired with guards of trains, stopped somewhere in open country between stations, entered the cars and demanded ten or fifteen rubles as
payment on each sack. After collecting their 'payment' they would drive
the train to some stop — rarely used — force the peasants to get out and
leave them on the bare platform, waiting hopelessly . . .

People waited in this way for a week or more, hungry and without
shelter. They became ill and died there, by the stop. Their fate concerned nobody, they were alien and unwanted even in their own country.

If, by some chance, these people managed once more to get on a train,
they had only further robbery to expect, and a further wretched delay at
another stop.

I listened to pitiful tales such as these, and anxiety began to gnaw at
my heart. It was a terrible and a strange thing to hear all this from people
who already experienced it, who had seen all this and had barely
survived, and who now were starting out for a second time on this
fearful and dangerous journey.

Hunger, runs a Ukrainian folk proverb, *is not one's brother.*

2.

After seeing the wandering peasants and listening to their stories, I
expected to find Kiev terrible, disagreeable, more like one of those
dreaded camps from which no one returns.

But I was mistaken, as it happened. Kiev was not terrible at all. On
the contrary, it was gay, flooded with sunshine, decorated with flowers,
filled with the sounds of hooting cars, loudspeakers, the laughter of girls
and joyful shouts of children. Kiev did not experience famine and lived
the full and vigorous life of a big city.

But all this turned out to be merely on the surface, a first impression.

We, the agronomists, arriving for the course at the People's Commissariat for Agriculture, were accomodated at the former monastery of St.
Michael, now transformed into the students' hostel. We used to lunch at
a restaurant not far from St. Sophia Square, but we had to buy bread and
other foods for breakfast and supper ourselves.

In the spring of 1933 only the villages of Ukraine were starving.
Towns, in spite of everything, were supplied with food, though not quite
in sufficient quantities. There was certainly no famine. Bread was sold
without ration cards, though one person might only buy about two
pounds of bread at one time.

The lines for bread were enormous. In one of the wings of the former monastery of St. Michael was a baker's shop. The line for bread used to reach almost to Khreshchatyk, the main thoroughfare of Kiev. Five assistants were working in the shop, but I was never able to buy bread there after less than two hours' wait.

One day while waiting in this line, I realized that Kiev was not really as gay as it had seemed to me on my first day there. The centrally-planned food supply to the town was not working well. Since peasants in the suburban villages were themselves starving they could not, of course, supply the urban markets with any produce.

As a result the majority of townspeople had to live only on what was supplied to the shops, but in the shops there was in fact very little. Bread was the only hope, but to obtain it whole families had to stand in line: father, mother, son, daughter, had each to wait their turn, since so little was given to one person.

Starving peasants were streaming into the town on foot and by train or other means. The shopkeepers were strictly forbidden to sell bread to these peasants.

And further, the so-called Ukrainian government, working through press and radio, incited the townspeople against the peasants. It was these latter, they said, who had been sabotaging production, and had thus created difficulties in the country. Kossior* himself, in one of his speeches, alleged that in 1932 about two hundred million poods of grain had perished in the Ukrainian fields.

He, Kossior, liked to quote Stalin whether the quotation was to the point or not. But for once he had forgotten the words of his patron, words uttered in January of that year, 1933, at the combined plenary session of the Central Committee and the Central Control Committee of the C.P.S.U.

" . . . If there is any question of responsibility and of guilt, then the responsibility rests wholly and entirely with the Communists, and the guilty party in everything is us, we, the Communists." (*Pravda*, January 17, 1933).

The Kievans believed neither the papers, nor the radio, nor Kossior. They helped the peasants as much as they could; they gave them free sleeping accommodation in their own houses, defended them from the police, and insisted that the shopkeepers should sell them bread if they stood in the line.

I remember the following incident: in front of me in the bread line was

---

General Secretary of the C.P.(B) of Ukraine.

a peasant woman, clothed in a scarf, a rough coat, high boots, and so on. It was plain she was not used to town life.

Suddenly a truck full of militiamen drove up to the line for a raid (razzia) on the peasants.

In a moment the Kievan women had surrounded the "auntie," helped her off with her scarf and rough coat, and put on her one of their town coats — had transformed her into a townswoman!

When the militiamen departed, the country woman told the Kievans with tears how in her village, once the prosperous and famous Trypillia, the Communists were destroying the walls of houses, ruining stores, digging under the floors, searching everywhere for bread-grain.

"They have ruined our village," she lamented, "forced people to wander about the country, and now we are not even allowed to buy city bread with our own money . . . "

3.

Raids on peasants were carried out daily in Kiev. They were hunted like dogs, those toilers of the Ukrainian soil, and dispatched outside the city to "special" camps, about which I had heard while travelling to Kiev. Here people called them "death camps."

These "death camps" were ordinary huts, built of wooden boards, with bare plank beds or some old, much-used straw. The food was so scanty and so poor that people, exhausted by starvation, usually lasted less than a week after arrival.

Every night the bodies of the dead were hauled by wagons to the morgues at the city hospitals. From there the corpses were taken to the cemeteries where they were buried in common graves.

Such "death camps" existed not only near Kiev, but also near Kharkiv, Dnipropetrovsk, and the other large towns of Ukraine.

Several years later I happened to meet a professor of medicine. In the course of our conversation the year 1933 was mentioned, and he told me this:

"I was then working at the main clinic of Dnipropetrovsk, and had the misfortune of having to examine the bodies of the dead which were brought from the Dnipropetrovsk "death camps." At night N.K.V.D. lorries brought them and set them down in a heap in the mortuary." The professor also told me that at a special meeting of the medical staff it was strictly forbidden to give any medical assistance to the starving peasants who came to the town. They were, it was said, enemies of the Soviet State.

4.

In the course we received instruction daily from nine o'clock in the morning until two in the afternoon. These were ordinary lectures dealing with insect pests attacking sugar beet. On the blackboard, cross-sections of slanting ditches were drawn for us, methods of tilling were demonstrated, new chemical preparations were shown, sprinklers, cutters, and the like illustrated. At one time I was very interested in these things, but I have by now long since forgotten them.

Of the agronomists who attended the course I was the youngest. Most of the others were older people with considerable experience of life, and, undoubtedly, with their own opinions about current events. They were not interested in museums, did not frequent cinemas or theaters. They spent all their free time standing in line for bread.

There were some who managed to stand in three or four lines in one day and so to collect several loaves of bread. They cut this into slices, dried it, and packed it into linen-cloth sacks which they had specially prepared, and sent these to their parents, brothers, or friends. Being a young man of twenty, I did not do this, and later had occasion to regret it bitterly.

I spent a whole month in Kiev and at the beginning of July returned to my M.T.S. I was to get a new job, with better conditions and a higher salary. I was due for it but declined it.

At that very moment death overtook my mother who lived far away from me. I experienced the deepest grief. Neither career, nor money, nor personal friendship, mattered to me any more . . .

I left everything to visit the emptiness of my home and the fresh grave of my mother . . .

CHAPTER TWO

What I Have Heard From Eye-Witnesses

1. Preface

"Speak, speak! Inflame with anger the copula of the sky. Obscure it with the clouds of your grief, let there by lightning and thunder . . . "

M. KOTSIUBYNSKY

THE FAMINE AMONG the Ukrainian peasants, that crime of the Kremlin, has driven such deep furrows into the memory of our nation that volumes of horror stories could be collected about it.

Peasants show an extraordinarily vivid memory when recalling the events of the spring of 1933. They do not forget the names of those who died from starvation, they remember the exact number of victims, the names of the "activists" who confiscated the grain, and all other details, however minute, of those events.

Many peasants, as evidenced during the last war, had carefully put down in writing all that occurred from 1929 up to 1933. These records they locked up in wooden boxes, and buried in the ground.

I know of several instances during 1942 and 1943 of peasants unearthing these chronicles and offering them for publication to editors of provincial papers. Unfortunately, most of the editors were by now uninterested in those past years, and so these valuable chronicles received no publicity.

I have written down several accounts of the famine in the villages in the regions of Odessa and Vinnytsia, from accounts given me by peasants immediately after the events concerned — in 1934, when I visited these villages personally.

16

The stories about the Left-Bank Ukraine and Kiev province, in particular those about the famine in the villages where the greatest Ukrainian poet, Taras Shevchenko, had been born and had lived in the nineteenth century, I have taken from the accounts of people in exile — people who came from those localities.

Most of the material was written down in the Displaced Persons' Transit Camp at Muenster in Germany, in 1948. A great many of us, on our way to Britain, waited there for a whole month, staying at a huge barracks which was converted from a military motor garage.

As it was winter, there was nothing to do and the evenings were long and dull. To pass the time, people told stories about their own experiences. There were many peasants from Eastern Ukraine, and they recalled life under Soviet rule. I have recorded many an interesting item, together with eye-witness accounts of the famine of the spring of 1933.

For reasons of expedience, the material collected has been arranged, not according to the actual order in which it was supplied to me, nor according to the localities concerned, but in respect of subject-matter under the headings to be found below. Exceptions to this are the sections relating to the villages of Shevchenko's homeland.

Since reaching Great Britain I have received many letters from those who had previously told me their stories. These letters furnish as it were the continuation of our earlier conversations, and extracts from them are included below with the stories.

I should like to express my sincere gratitude to everyone who, by his letters or his stories, has helped me to collect this invaluable and interesting chapter.

Also I should like now to appeal to anyone who witnessed the famine in 1933 to write down his own recollections of it and to make them available for publication. Let the entire civilized world know what Communist rule has meant for millions of people.

II. Children

> "And there under the hedge
> A swollen child from hunger dies."
>
> T. Shevchenko

1.

". . . I was born in the village of Horbiv, 13 miles from Cherni-
hiv. At the beginning of collectivization I was seven and I started to go
to school.

We experienced starvation in 1933, also. My father and mother had
their limbs swollen. One of our neighbors died together with his wife
after eating green poppy seeds.

We also tried to eat various kinds of plants: corn stalks, elm seeds,
roots of wild carrot, parsnips, clover blossom, and so on. We tried
eating lupin. The spotted beans of this plant are as bitter as pepper, and
had to be cooked several times before it was possible to eat them. From
lupin we, especially the children, had stomach trouble.

A school teacher from the next village was floating dead in a boat on
the river about that time. He must have eaten some poisonous water
plant.

A woman went out of her mind with hunger. She used to catch
tadpoles in a pond and eat them. The children would not let her do this,
so she would weep and beg them for food. Later this woman died
outside the village among the weeds.

I myself saw an old woman, exhausted from starvation, wandering
across the fields with green ears of wheat under her arm. The chairman
of the kolhosp, "comrade" Rozhok, riding by on his horse, caught her,
beat her severely with his whip, and knocked her off her feet with his
horse . . .

In the last stages of the famine the hard grain delivery quota was
imposed on our household, so that we had to leave our home just before
winter.

A communist party member, F. Skyba, one eye blind, the other one
looking like the eye of a devil, would rush into a house, first of all seize
the holy ikons and then throw them with all his strength against the door
or threshold. Once, a mother said to him.

"Where shall I go with my children for the winter?"

"Go and drown them," was the savage rejoinder.
But later he himself died from tuberculosis.

Extract from the letter of V.K-1.

2.

In the village of Stepanivka, near Vinnytsia, the kolhosp wagons did
not pick up the bodies of those dead people who had not been members
of the kolhosp. A widowed woman carried her three children in a linen
sheet to the cemetery and later died herself.

In the same village a woman died in one house and left two small children. When the wagon drove up, the dead body of the mother was picked up, but the children were left in the empty house without any bread, care or supervision at all.

3.

In the village of Petropavlivka, near Dnipropetrovsk, a young peasant farmer, dispossessed as a kurkul and expelled from the village in 1929, secretly returned in the spring of 1933 to his village.

He came on foot at night from the railway station, but was afraid to enter the village. In front of his former house, where his old parents were now living, was a rye-field, with the rye just sprouting. He lay down in it and fell asleep.

In the morning, when the sun rose, he saw the following scene: a girl of fourteen, the daughter of Omelko Slyzky, his former neighbor, had dragged out the body of her father from her house and was trying to lift it on a cart. Barefooted, clad only in a shirt, the tears streaming from her eyes, she could not manage to raise the heavy body.

"I came out from the rye," the man told me, "and asked: 'Where are you taking your father?'

" 'To the cemetery,' the girl replied, 'he has been lying dead for three days in the house, and I am afraid to sleep with him here!' "

4.

As a result of mass mortality during the month of May, in the villages and towns of Ukraine shadow-like flocks of hungry orphan children roamed about. The "sympathetic administration" started to set up children's homes in the villages and small towns.

A former inmate of such a "home" relates his experiences:

". . . My father had his body swollen and died of starvation. My mother, exhausted from hunger, on her way home from the field one day, pulled two beetroots on the kolhosp field. A Communist foreman overtook her on his horse and gave her such a beating that she scarcely managed to get back home, and two days later she died.

"We, two orphans — I, ten years old; and my sister, six — were taken to an orphanage. The spring that year was cold and rainy. The orphanage consisted of an old peasant house with broken windows. All of us slept on linen bedspreads, without any coverings. The children were freezing at night and, lacking proper food, they soon became ill and died.

"The nurse put spades into the hands of us older children, led us to the cemetery and ordered us to dig graves. We would dig out a shallow pit, not more than two feet deep. The nurse would put the bare body of a dead child on a linen sheet for four of us to lift by the corners and take to the cemetery. The corpse was dropped into the pit and some earth thrown on top of it.

"In this way I carried my own sister to the grave and covered her with earth. Now, in exile, I wait for that moment when it will be possible for me to carry to the cemetery those who gave me such a happy childhood."

5.

". . . In the spring of 1933," relates a former peasant, now a refugee in Britain, "my father carried corpses in a wagon to the cemetery. He was not a member of the kolhosp, and as a punishment for being an "Indus*," he was ordered to collect the dead. It so happened that he had to carry away one of his own cousins, the latter's wife and their son, that is, his nephew. But the boy was still alive and might have been saved.

"But he still lives," cried my father.

"Da shto-zhe my za nim eshcho raz budem ekhat. Vse ravno zdokhnit. Davay!" (in Russian. But what's the use of having to come for him a second time. He will die anyway. Come on!) said the "ten-thousander" who was also chairman of the collective farm.

In the cemetery, all the bodies of the dead were tossed onto a heap in one common grave, and that boy was laid on the top of them. He lay there, still living, for three days. . ."

6.

In the village of Rudkivtsi in Kamianets-Podillia province, two children were born in 1932, and one in 1933. The total population was 1460 persons.

---

* "Indus" from Indian, a nickname for a peasant who remained an individual farmer, refusing to become a member of the kolhosp.

III. In the Homeland of Taras Shevchenko

> "The village looks as if burnt down by fire."
>
> T. SHEVCHENKO

"I HEAR THAT you are talking about the year '33. In our country things happened that God should forbid."

"Where do you come from?"

"I'm from Kyrylivka in the district of Vilshansky. Ever heard of it?"

"Isn't that where Shevchenko was born?"

"No, he was born in Moryntsi — the village next to ours. I was working there, I knew all the villages. There is one called Zelena Dibrova, and there, out of 1210 households, only 367 remained."

"And the rest — the people died?"

"Some died, others escaped, and the village became almost deserted. There is another called Borovykivka, where 123 households survived out of more than six hundred. The village of Tarasivka in the district of Zvenyhorodka is deserted now. In Moryntsi itself four hundred houses became vacant, and in Kyrylivka only a half remained."

"Was not the memory of Taras Hryhorovych* at least respected?"

"What — they . . . respect! People were carried off to the cemetery there just as anywhere else, several bodies in a wagon. Activists were even found here, too, among our own people. They served well enough, until they themselves . . . "

And T-ko went on to tell us how in the village of Moryntsi the foreman of the kolhosp "brigade," Petro Tkachenko, in order to save time for more fruitful journeys of the wagon, insisted on the transport to the cemetery of all those already too weak to stand. "They'll die in any case, so why stand on ceremony," he would say. His obedient agents did as they were ordered, and later they carried Tkachenko away himself to the same common grave.

"In Vilshana, in the kolhosp "The Red Way," Fedir Tynyka of the fifth "brigade" threw into the grave an old woman, Olena Vakulenko. She was still alive at the time he, beast that he was, tossed her into the grave. All the blame for this rests upon Anikin Musienko, a party man, who was in charge of the removal of the dead to the cemetery."

---

*Shevchenko

" . . . The spring that year was rainy," our companion continued, "and weeds grew to the height of a man. By the roadside, between Kyrylivka and Budyshcha, in the orrach near the Budyshcha pond, at the end of June were found the bodies of two children — one about seven years old and the other perhaps ten. Who knows whose children they were? No body seemed to have missed them, no one asked for them, they perished like kittens . . . "

IV. The Fate of Some Families

"Life has become easier, life has become more joyful, comrades!"

J. STALIN

1.

THE VILLAGE OF Orikhove near Zhytomyr numbered over 30 households before the famine, but after 1933 a mere third of the houses were still inhabited — the rest standing vacant. There were families who died out completely. For example, the Tarasiuk family which had consisted of seven souls, all of whom died. The Sventsitsky family — with six people; the Sokolovsky — with five members; that of Fedir Triletsky — with five people; of Yakiv Herasymiv — with ten; of Yarema Vdovychenko — with twelve; and of Pylyp Maydanovych — with eight, and so on.

Particularly tragic was the fate of the Viitovych family. Their youngest son, sixteen years old, was returning one day from school at Shakhvorivka by way of Marianivka village, when he died on his way home by the roadside. He was buried there on the spot. The elder daughter, Palazhka, died in the kolhosp field. The old mother died in the street on her way to work in the kolhosp. The father's body was found in the Korostyhiv forest, half-devoured by beasts.

Their eldest son, Semen Viitovych, was a chief of the N.K.V.D. in the Far East, in the city of Vladivostok. After the harvest of 1933 he came to visit his family, but found an empty house, densely overgrown with weeds. He spent three days at Orikhove making inquiries about his parents, his brother and his sister. Then he returned to Vladivostok. What kind of an N.K.V.D. man was he after that visit? We cannot tell . . . "

2.

Another participant in the conversation told the following story about the same village of Orikhove:

" . . . One day I was walking home from town, when I saw — sitting down not far from the road under a fir-tree — Maria Prylutska, a widow. I called out to her:

"Come, Maria, let us walk together."

She did not reply, and I came closer to her. She was dead. Evidently she had been eating as she died, for she held a piece of bread from clover blossom in her hand. She must have sat down to eat and died there under the fir-tree, leaving four children waiting at home."

3.

In the village of Kucha in the Nova-Ushytsia district of Kamianets-Podillia lived an honest and thrifty farmer called Semen Bilokin. He had a family of six, five hectares (about equal to 12½ acres), two horses, two cows, and ten sheep. He refused to join the kolhosp and was therefore a kurkul. As his farm was listed in the kurkul category, he had to fulfill a heavy quota in deliveries of grain and meat. He accomplished this. Then they imposed on him a "plan for the household." But he had nothing left with which to complete this. As a reprisal his property was confiscated and all his family expelled from the house.

In the spring of 1933, his wife, daughter, and one son died from starvation. His youngest son, a child of four, was taken into the care of an uncle. Bilokin himself and his eldest son survived, but were deported to Archangel. The father died in exile in the north, and the son returned to his village in 1942. No one knows what has become of him now.

4.

In the hamlet of Stepanivski Khutory near Voronovychy in Podillia, lived another thrifty farmer called Mykhailo D-ko. He had a nice house, a pair of horses and a cow. He did not join the kolhosp; he was a kurkul, too. When the "household plan" was imposed upon him, he could not fullfil its demands. The secretary of the local party committee (a newcomer from Russia) ordered the requisitioning of all the grain he possessed, also of the horses and the cow, leaving him only the house.

In the spring of 1933 his wife and three children died from hunger. His own body swollen, completely weakened, Mykhailo met the secretary and said to him:

"You have achieved your aim already. I have buried my wife and children."

"Eto khorosho," (in Russian: That's fine) said the secretary. "You will die too and your house will come in handy for our kolhosp."

"You won't live to see that day, you dog!" cried Mykhailo and went home. There he soaked a rag in lamp oil, lit it and threw it on the thatched roof of his house. When the entire roof had caught fire, Mykhailo entered the house, lay down on the bench and was burnt to death in his house.

V. Terrible Statistics

"Of bodies dead, you, purple hecatombs."
YURII KLEN

1.

" . . . AS FOR MYSELF, I was employed as a statistician in the administration of the Mezhybizh district of Vinnytsia province. I visited a lot of the villages. Some of the information I obtained I carry with me even now.

"The village of Shrubky, for instance. There five people were shot for failing to deliver grain, and this number includes three men and two women. Also there, thirty-nine people were deported to Siberia.

"The village of Matkivtsi, where there were 312 households, and a population of 1293. Three men and two women were shot for cutting off ears of corn in their own garden-plots; 24 families were deported to Siberia. In the spring of 1933 a part of the population fled from the village, while part died out and the village then became completely deserted. A black flag was hung up in that village as a sign that the village was sealed. In the registers an entry was made. It read: "This village died out from typhus."

"The village of Khodakivtsi in the Proskuriv district had 263 housholds and a population of 1228. Two men and one woman were shot. The village, however, lost 613 people — most of them having died in the famine.

"In the village of Hrynivtsi there were 283 households, with 2029 inhabitants. A woman, named Hanka — I have forgotten her surname — was shot for cutting off some ears of grain in her own garden. Forty families were deported to Siberia. The village lost 792 of its people — most of them dying in the famine.

"The village of Veremiyivka in the Krasyliv district of Vinnytsia province had 128 households and 1210 inhabitants. Thirteen families were deported to Siberia. How many people the village lost as a result of the famine I do not know.

"In Slobidka Krasylivska 68 people were deported, many died, but I do not know the exact numbers.

"I saw with my own eyes an N.K.V.D. man kill a woman and strike down an eight-year-old child — for plucking some green peas in a field . . . "

From the letter of Yakym R-uk.

2.

" . . . The village of Dukhanivka in the Borivsky district of Cherni-hiv province numbered over 800 households and a population of 3240. How many died in the famine of 1933 I do not know, but I have with me a list of families who died out completely." (There follows a list of names with the numbers of people against each name) "25 families were sent beyond the Urals from that village. One third of the total number of houses were left vacant . . . "

From the letter of S. Ya-ky.

3.

About the village of Rudkivtsi in the Nova-Ushytsia district, F. H-ko says the following:

" . . . In our village, from a total of 1460 inhabitants, 338 people died in the spring of 1933, the majority of them men. In 1932 twelve families were deported to Siberia.

"During the twenty years of the Soviet regime, about one third of the village population passed through prison. Neither I nor my father re-member anyone from our village serving a prison sentence before the revolution . . . "

4.

In the village of Antonivka near Bila Tserkva one street was com-pletely liquidated, because in the spring of 1933 everyone there died in the famine.

"I have heard that your village is famous for apples. Is it true?"

"Well, this was so once, but now everything there looks as if scorched by fire."

5.

In the village of Ozarentsi of the Kamianets-Podillia province, lived only Protestants. After the spring of 1933 only a handful to them remained — most of them had died.

In the village of Halaikivtsi in the Kurylivka district people were buried in a ravine. The corpses were heaped up there and covered with lime.

From the village of Dyakivka in the Vinnytsia-Podolia province, 54 families — 234 people — were deported to Siberia and to the Murmansk area.

6.

"In the spring of 1933 I was working as a statistician in the village of Chornyn in Kiev province," says V-ko. "According to a directive from the district, it was forbidden to reveal that people had died from starvation. One was told to write: 'Died from infectious disease.'"

VI. The "International"

1.

"We'll grate to dust all our betrayers."
FROM A UKRAINIAN TEXT

S-IUK RELATES: IN our village a foreman of the kolhosp came to one of my neighbors to call him to work. The latter was busy grinding some grains of barley to obtain flour. He had to do this by hand, for the flour-mills were closed and there was no quern to hand. He put a few grains on a small stone and then ground it with another stone.

"What are you doing?" asked the foreman.

"Well," he replied, "I am going to grate to dust all our betrayers!"

2.

"Get up, arise, you working people . . . "
FROM THE INTERNATIONALE

In the village of Stepanivka near Vinnytsia there lived an "activist" called Matvyi. He was extremely fond of the "Internationale." He would go about the village as a member of a commission, confiscate bread-grain, and sing: "Get up, arise, you working people!" Naturally the villagers nicknamed him "Get up arise."

This was in autumn. In the spring of 1933, however, when the rye was just blossoming, I was walking home from the town one day with a relative of mine. As we passed along a field we wondered whether we should live to eat bread made from that rye . . .

Then we saw him. By the roadside, ad the end of a field, there was Matvyi lying with his nose on the ground. We came up to him and called out:

"Eh, Matvyi, get-up, arise!"

He raised his head, looked at us, and then once more his nose touched the ground. There, by the rye-field, he died . . .

VII. Punished for Pulling a Few Ears of Wheat

> "The henchmen — betrayers — torment us."
> T. SHEVCHENKO

1.

IN THE VILLAGE of Shliakhova, Maria Havryliuk was sentenced to ten years penal servitude in a distant labor camp for cutting a hundred ears of ripening wheat on her own field, not even on that belonging to the kolhosp. Two weeks earlier her husband had died from starvation.

2.

At Olenivka, a village of the Zakhariv district near Odessa, Ivan Bondarenko, the father of four children, was sentenced to ten years imprisonment. His whole crime consisted in cutting some ears of grain in his own field.

3.

In Veremiyivka village near Poltava after the 1933 harvest, according to Pylyp Sh-y, Hryhoriy Lepetukha, aged 23, the son of a dispossessed peasant, was gathering ears of corn in the kolhosp field which had already been harvested and was waiting for the plough.

A kolhosp watchman, called Kanivets, and ardent "activist," saw Lepetukha, rode after him on his horse and beat him to death. The killer was not brought to trial.

VIII. Cannibalism

> "Glassy, almost half-frozen eyes
> Of mothers who their babies own
> From hunger devour . . ."
>
> YURII KLEN

YA-YN FROM THE region of Sumy has given us the following account: "Once I had to go to the village of Dibrova to find a wagon to transport some hay. I found two brothers there who were willing to do the work for me and we agreed upon terms. I then took them with me to show them where the hay was.

As we walked through the village, one of them said to me:

"Look at this cottage. Yesterday a mother butchered her child here. The meat was still half-cooked in the oven, when her elder daughter ran out to the children in the street and said: 'We shall be having meat today.'

"The children asked: 'But where did you get it?'

" 'Mother has killed Mysha, it's being cooked now.'

"When the children told this to their parents, the neighbors began to collect by the house. The woman saw the people gathering, and grasped the girl by the hand, hurrying her into the house, and snatching the meat out of the oven. She started to eat it herself and shoved it into the girl's hand.

"But at this moment the neighbors broke into the house and prevented them finishing their meal. That same day police arrived and took the woman away to the district town."

O. Stepovy, in addressing the Ukrainian Community in London on Whit Sunday, 1948, spoke thus:

" . . . The horror of the hellish mass famine of the Ukrainian peasants cannot be described in words.

"Hard as you may try, Ladies and Gentlemen, to imagine these horrors, you can never conceive them as they were in reality. This may be so because the mind of a normal human being is unable to picture to himself that degree of suffering from starvation, when a mother consumes the corpse of her own child . . . "

IX. "Red Kurkuls"

> "We fought for the land, but did not bargain for the crop."
> MODERN UKRAINIAN PROVERB

1.

"WHAT DO I remember about my village? Clearly, many poor peasants perished in the Murmansk region and Siberia, some even of those who were formerly activists and red partisans.

There lived a certain Karpo Poshtyrian in our village. Before the revolution he was a rather poor but independent peasant. Together with his father he supported the Soviet regime actively. He was opposed to Petliura and Hetman Skoropadsky. He enriched himself as a result of the revolution, received three hectares — about 7½ acres — of land belonging to a big landowner and to the Church. In 1929 he committed suicide because he could not cope with the payment of taxes and the grain deliveries, which were considered to be the first stage in the attack on the kurkul.

Mykhailo Tkachuk killed himself in 1931. During the Revolution he was on the side of the Bolsheviks, but was later on tried for taking part in an anti-collectivization rising which took place in our village."*

Opanas Mosiuk, Ivan Produn, Yakym Produn, Hryhory Nahorniak, Hryhir Hnatiuk, Kyrylo Kulyk, Yakym Moskovchuk — were all deported with their families to the Murmansk area in 1932. All of them were among the first soviet activists before collectivization; they had plundered the property of big landowners, of the Church, and of the

---

* The village Rudkivtsi in Podolia.

public. But when faced with the prospect of joining the kolhosp they refused, were all dispossessed, and deported. All of them died near Murmansk.

Petro Tkach, V. Semeniuk, and Arsen Handziuk were formerly red partisans in the division of Kotovsky. They all came from Bessarabia but stayed to live in our village. They could not go home because they had taken part in a rising against Rumania. All of them opposed collectivization and perished as "enemies of the people" at the hands of bolsheviks.

I am not now writing about kurkuls, but only about poor peasants. Neither am I including anything about those who perished in 1937."

Exact from the letter of R-r H-ch.

2.

" . . . The village of Bernashivka in the Yaryshiv district: Yustyn Voityshyn, Ivan Melnyk, both former Soviet revolutionaries and opponents of the Ukrainian liberation movement, also perished as "red kurkuls."

You know yourself that every village has on average thirty houses standing vacant, because those who lived in them were either deported or exterminated . . . and who can write about it all? . . .

From the letter of Hanch-k.

3.

In the village of Lytvynovychi, near Chernihiv, Pavlo Vashchenko, formerly a landless peasant, enriched himself during the Soviet rule. Later, in 1930, he was deported with his family to Siberia as a kurkul.

Kyrylo Rud' was a village shepherd before the revolution, as also was his son. He did not possess any land of his own. During the revolution he was an activist; he was given a plot of land and grew prosperous. He was sent to Siberia in 1930 as a kurkul.

4.

In the village of Sharpivka near Poltava lived a certain Makar Sheremet, a village shepherd. He became rich during the revolution and, in 1930, was deported as a kurkul.

5.

Stepan Marchuk lived in the village of Veremiyivka, in the Krasyliv district near Vinnytsia. Before the revolution he did not own even as much land as would suffice for a garden. During the revolution he was a "red partisan." The Bolsheviks gave him five hectares* of land and in 1930 they dispossessed him and deported him to Siberia as a red kurkul.

In the same village there also lived Herasym Arkhypovych, who owned half a hectare of land before the revolution. Not only he, but also his wife, Paraska, were activists. She was one of the first Soviet deputies in the early days of the revolution, and a well-known activist in the Krasyliv district. In 1930 they were both dispossessed and deported to Siberia . . .

X. When Thieves Have power . . .

1.

IN OUR VILLAGE, writes Kh. P-ch, a party member, Mykhailo Lysiak, came with other members of a commission to dispossess his own father-in-law. He listed all the property and first of all confiscated all grain.

When the wagon had gone off laden with grain, and the other members of the commission were on the point of leaving, Lysiak delayed them and climbed up to the loft. He did not find anything there except some boards of pine which he began to throw down into the yard.

"What are you doing, Mykhailo?" his brother-in law asked him. "Father put those boards there ready for his coffin."

"I don't care about that," said Lysiak, "let him die all the sooner. We'll bury him without a coffin,"

2.

In the village of Veremiyivka near Poltava there lived a communist, Nykyfor Kostyria. When his wife bore him twins, two boys, he gave them nicknames instead of serious ones. He called one of them Marx, the other Engels.

At the time of delivering grain to the state, Kostyria was the scourge of the whole village. In the spring, as people were suffering severely from swellings and dying from hunger, he used to say:

"Praise be to you, Marx and Engels, the sinners against communism are dying at last!"

---

* Once hectare is equal roughly to 2½ acres.

One day Kostyria came to the house of a kurkul and began to question him.

"What are you eating? Why are you not yet swelling up? Eh? Now tell me."

The farmer began to excuse himself as ingeniously as he could, but the inspired builder of socialism would not believe the kurkul and made a thorough search of the house. He found what he was looking for: at the very bottom of the box, the "class enemy" has hidden — as if it were a priceless treasure — a small bag of flour mingled with finely ground bark and leaves.

Kostyria confiscated the "bread surplus" found in possession of this kurkul. He carried it outside into the street and poured it into a pool . . .

3.

In the village of Chornyn near Kiev a communist youth, Maichenko, met his mother-in-law, wife of old Horbach, in the street. He took her shoes and her fur-coat away, because, as he put it, she was a kurkul's wife.

4.

In the village of Fedorivka near Rostov, in 1932, peasants used to be taken and shut up together in a cellar. Smoke was then let into the unventilated room. When the people began to choke and to suffocate, they were let out and were asked: "Now, have you remembered where you have hidden your grain?"

XI. There Were Others, Too

"Escape, escape, don't try to save your life
But save your soul . . . "

YURII KLEN

IN MAY 1933, the district party committee of Krasny Kut sent a communist youth called Varhula to the village of Murafa near Kharkiv, as an authorized agent in charge of meat deliveries.

Varhula came to the village and visited some houses. He saw people suffering from dropsy and dying from hunger. He went to the village council office, rang up the secretary of the district party committee himself, and said to him:

"I can fulfill your quota of meat deliveries, not with pigs or cows, but — with human corpses."

After such a statement, Varhula had to make good his escape as fast as his legs could carry him . . .

XII. The Activists

1.

IN STEPANIVKA VILLAGE, an activist, Denys Andrusiak, was an ardent "grain-deliverer." He was famous throughout the autumn for his skill in detecting grain even in the water — on the bottom of a river, for instance. In the spring, however, he was brought to hospital, suffering from swellings, but so honored was he that he was not even given a dish to eat from. He went home to fetch one, and on the way he stumbled, and did not rise up again . . .

2.

In the village of Vilshana near Kiev a former red partisan, Omelko Nesterenko, squeezed out the last grain of wheat from the peasants. In the spring of 1933 his own body swelled and he died from starvation.

3.

In the village of Berezova in the Kurylivka district, from among a total population of 2300, about 600 died in the famine. I the revolution this village had sympathized with Bolsheviks. The red partisan Struk originated there. It was he who later organized a kolhosp in Berezova, then removed the bells from the church tower and attacked religion.

But in the spring of 1933 some young activists, pupils of his, saw where his "activity" had led the village. They chopped off his head and left a note with it, saying: "That's for you, for the kolhosp!"

4.

Fedir Hordievych relates as follows: "In our vilage, there was a red partisan, Ilko Bushovsky. He persecuted cruelly all who had sympathized with the Hetman movement — the Ukrainian monarchists — in 1918. He used to beat people to death for their Hetmanite sympathies.

When the drive started for collectivization, he refused to join the kolhosp. "The friends of collectivization" beat him wtih sticks on the head in broad daylight. As they beat him they said:

"This is your communism, Bushovsky!"

Then one day a party of former red partisans bound their former leader, Bushovsky, with a rope and, throwing it over a beam, pulled him up by it.

Later he complained to one of my neighbors that even his own daughter would not let him into her house. "No one knows me any more!" he lamented.

Old and sick, he used to carry firewood to the town in a sack, sell it, and live on the proceeds. In the spring of 1933 he died from starvation under a hedge.''

5.

In the village of Rudkivtsi, a certain Marian Panko was chairman of the village council. Earlier he had been chairman of the "Komnezam" — the committee of poor peasants. In the spring of 1933 he died from hunger, and so also did his wife and two daughters . . .

6.

In Khodakivtsi, a village in the Proskuriv district, a former red partisan called Ivan Pavluk died from starvation in the spring of 1933. In 1927 he had been chairman of the local collective farm.

7.

In the village of Diakivka near Vinnytsia, the following active supporters of bolshevism died the hungry death: Martyn Rozikovsky, Semen Tsymbaliuk, Parfirii Valasenko. All of them had occupied leading posts in local affairs at one time or another, but yet in the spring of 1933 they did not escape their cup of bitterness.

8.

In Dukhanivka, a village near Chernihiv, a former red partisan and member of the Communist Party, who was also chief organizer of the dispossession of kurkuls in that village, died from starvation.

Do not dig a hole under your neighbor, lest you fall into it yourself! So runs a popular saying. It is one we should remember, and perhaps above all the communist and bolshevik activists should bear it in mind . . .

XIII. The "Leaders" Saw for Themselves

1.

In JUNE, 1933, when the famine reached its climax, Hryhory Ivanovych Petrovsky, then Prime Minister of the puppet "government" of Ukraine, and nicknamed as the "All-Ukrainian Elder," came on a visit to the village of Kovalivka in the district of Nemyriv.

This "leader" walked silently through the village. He saw people with their bodies swollen from hunger, he saw them dying, and he saw those who were already dead. But that spectacle did not prevent him from enjoying a good dinner with the manager of the local sugar-beet factory, and from returning, as if nothing particular had happened, to his office.

No easing of the peasants' lot resulted from that visit!

2.

In the little town of Kalius in the Nova-Ushytsia district Volodymyr Zatonsky came in June 1933 for a visit. He was chairman of the "workers' and peasants' inspection."

A crowd of several hundred peasants, exhausted by starvation, came to see the "leader."

The secretary of the district committee of the Communist Party said to Zatonsky: "Eto te, kotorye ne khotiat rabotat'." (In Russian: These are the ones who do not want to work.)

"Well," remarked Zatonsky, who could actually speak Ukrainian, "if they die, it will be a lesson to others!"

In the autumn of 1933, to the little town of Kozelshchyna near Kharkiv, came no less a person than Molotov himself — as representative of the Central Committee of the Communist Party in charge of grain deliveries. A special railway branch line was built for him leading off the Kharkiv-Odessa main line.

Viacheslav Mikhailovich (Molotov) was sitting in a saloon-coach and briefing the local party leaders.

It seems that he gave them a good briefing, because in the spring of 1933 in this very town of Kozelshchyna over a thousand peasants died from starvation.

These victims are a direct burden on the conscience of Molotov.

XIVI. New Settlers

> "On the cossacks' corpses free,
> On the robbed corpses!"
>   T. SHEVCHENKO

THE MAJORITY OF the inhabitants of the village of Chornyn in the district of Tarashcha near Kiev died from starvation in the spring of 1933.

Already in June, even before the harvest began, new settlers arrived from the central regions of Muscovy. The Russian newcomers started by dragging out the dead bodies of our Ukrainian peasants from their houses to bury them nearby, as they were in a hurry to take possession as soon as possible of their new living quarters.

The Russian immigrants did not starve at all: they were receiving a special "immigrants' ration" of about 50 pounds of wheat flour per month each.

The Ukrainian population reproached the Russian strangers for taking advantage of the fearful tragedy of the Ukrainian peasants, but the Russians exculpated themselves by saying that they were told to go and settle on the vacant land by government representatives in Moscow. "You are needed there," they had been urged.

But some of them, whose conscience had not quite been extinguished, in particular some peasants from the Tambov region, returned to Muscovy.

2.

The population of Murafa in the Krasny Kut district near Kharkiv, died out in the famine, but some children survived and were taken care of by activists.

New settlers — Russians — arrived in the deserted village and occupied the empty houses. One day, in the autumn of that same year, 1933, the orphan-children attacked the children of the Russian strangers. They beat them up, shouting at them:

"You have murdered our parents by hunger, and occupied our houses. Go away from our homes! Go away from our villages!"

The schoolmaster of the local school, Stetsiura, was tried and sentenced as responsible for this incident to twelve years hard labor. He was accused of having failed to explain to his pupils the real significance of the arrival of the new settlers, and to implant in the children the love of the "fraternal Russian people" . . .

CHAPTER THREE

The Bosses Are Satisfied

'You may now rejoice, oh, hangman,
Oh, you cursed! You cursed one!''
T. SHEVCHENKO

IN JANUARY 1934, two congresses, one after the other, took place in Kiev and Moscow. In Kiev the congress of the Communist Party of Ukraine was held, and in Moscow the congress of the All-Union Communist Party.

At these meetings, the "bosses" — both the "Little Russian" quislings and the Muscovites — boasted of great successes in the "glorious" year of 1933.

1.

"You, henchmen, slaves and Moscow's mud.''
T. SHEVCHENKO

The general secretary of the C.P.(B) of Ukraine, Stanislav Kossior, declared:

" . . . Only in 1933, under direct leadership of the Central-Committee of the C.P.S.U., under the leadership of Comrade Stalin and following his directives, we, in Ukraine, have carried out the struggle for the detection of nationalist deviations in the C.P.U., the struggle against counter-revolutionary elements, and against nationalism in general. Everyone knows now from experience how urgent was the need for a universal and ruthless fight against such nationalist deviation, inadequately resisted until the present time. And the fact that we have smashed nationalism, that we have now started to perform our work in the villages properly, *has actually gained the success of the year 1933* . . . "

The Deputy Prime Minister, Panas Liubchenko, said:

" . . . Only one year has passed, the glorious year 1933. With the

37

strengthening of its leadership, the C.P.U. has regrouped its ranks, raised its fighting ability, smashed nationalist deviation headed by Skrypnyk,* smashed Petliura's nationalist nests in agricultural, cultural and other organizations. The Ukrainian nationalists and their masters abroad will long remember the Cheka and the G.P.U. of the Soviet Ukraine.''

There happened to be another "glorious" year in Ukraine, the year 1937, but Panas Liubchenko did not have the nerve to live it through. He shot himself. Apparently the Cheka and the G.P.U. of Soviet Ukraine had reminded him of something . . .

A delegate to the congress of the C.P.(B) of Ukraine, Lytvyn, boasted thus: " . . . In this way in 1933 the C.P.U. has carried out *a great work*, purging our organizations of nationalist elements and of Petliurists . . . ''

The chief of the G.P.U. in Ukraine, the executioner directly responsible, V. Balytsky, said; " . . . In 1933 the fist of the G.P.U. hit out in two directions: first at the kurkul and Petliurist elements in the villages . . . , and secondly at the leading centers of nationalism . . . ''

The Prime Minister of the Soviet Ukraine, Hryhory Petrovsky, said at the 17th congress of the C.P.U.:

" . . . It was very difficult for us to expose failings in the national front. Earlier we had criticized the work of the Central Committee of the C.P.U. and of the Party as a whole, in respect of nationalist-deviationist elements. Some time ago, the C.P.U., headed by Kaganovich, repelled those attacks. More recently, however, the nationalist elements could not be so easily kept in check. The assistance of the C.P.S.U. Central Committee, in sending us trusty comrades, was timely. We are now in control and can liquidate shortcomings on the economic front, while the G.P.U., headed by Comrade Balytsky, has unmasked and liquidated the counter-revolution . . . ''

It appears that the C.P.U. of itself was not able to deal with nationalist elements, and it was the assistance from Moscow that saved the situation. This assistance, was Petrovsky himself said, was forthcoming from the first, Kaganovich earlier on, and Balytsky later, as "boss,'' each having only his own people to help him.

---

* Minister of Education.

After all these declarations and speeches one is reminded of the words of our great Taras Shevchenko:

> "Why are you vainly boasting, you,
> The sons of the heart-grieved Ukraine!
> That better in the yoke you walk,
> Than your fathers did the same?"

2.

Pavel Postyshev, a Russian, sent specially into Ukraine in January 1933; now boasted, after one year in office, of his achievements. He delivered several speeches in public. The most interesting of these for us are those of November 1933 and of January 1934.

In the first of these, Postyshev spoke, among other things, about Ukrainian culture, or — to be more exact — about nationalism in Ukrainian culture, He said:

" . . . Surely it is a fact that in the 1933 edition of the history of Ukrainian Culture, one reads: "Notwithstanding all her relations with Asia, Ukraine, from ancient times until today, has been a cultural corner of Europe, and it is impossible to understand her culture and her arts without connecting them with the culture and art of Europe . . . "

He, Postyshev, pretended not to know that no Ukrainian scholar or artist could think otherwise than this. Although Postyshev boasted that he had smashed the Ukrainian Academy of Science — and how many times had this not been done already! — he was not succeeding in severing Ukraine from Europe, just as no one else had succeeded in this.

In the second speech, Postyshev gave a chronological account of the nationalist movement in Ukraine, of course from the communist point of view. This is what he said:

" . . . The attempt of the Union for the Liberation of Ukraine was a serious sign for the C.P.U. We learned from this that the Ukrainian nationalist counter-revolution has begun to concentrate on her main work in the Soviet Ukraine, and that this work consisted mainly in trying to infiltrate personally wherever possible into every walk of social, economic and cultural life; into the Communist Party, and into Komsomol, with the aim of dominating the schools and using them to graft nationalist ideas on to the pupils' minds, and to select reliable cadres from students at the higher institutions of learning.

In 1933, the C.P.S.U. perceived a second sign — an extremely loud and alarming one. The so-called "Ukrainian National Center" was discovered. This consisted of a bloc of Ukrainian and Galician nationalist parties. Among the members of this organization were Chechel, Holubvych, Vasyl Mazurenko, Lyzanivsky, Khrystiuk, Yavorsky and others. This was a nationalist, fascist, combative organization which aimed at the unification of all the forces of the nationalist counter-revolution and preparation for a rising in Ukraine . . . ''

Balytsky then said about this organization that it was a bloc of the Ukrainian nationalist parties: the Ukrainian Communist Party, Borotbists (the militant section of the Socialist Party), Social-Revolutionaries, Social-Democrats and others. Kossior mentioned that Hrushevsky and Kossak belonged to this organization.

"Meanwhile," continued Postyshev, "the nationalist elements became particularly active in 1931 and 1932, penetrating into ever new branches of the socialist organization. In the beginning of 1933 the G.P.U. discovered a new organization — the "Ukrainian Military Organization."

Moscow's *Pravda*, on January 18, 1933, summed up the activity of Postyshev. After describing the character of the political situation in Ukraine in 1933, and without mentioning the famine by so much as one word — for this paper is *Pravda** all right! — it stated that, thanks to new leadership, the Central Committee of the C.P.U. and the Party had begun to function better, and therefore had achieved *great successes.''*

"This victory," said *Pravda,* "must be ascribed to the assistance and direct leadership of the Central Committee of the C.P.S.U., and also the personal interest of Comrade Stalin in the matter."

"But," went on *Pravda,* "notwithstanding the fact that the class enemy had been defeated, he would try to sabotage, wreck, and fight . . . Counter-revolutionary nationalism had been smashed, but the danger from national chauvinism continued to exist in Ukraine."

The last statement of *Pravda* is indeed true, because the nationalist movement in Ukraine has existed and will go on existing until the Ukrainian people are free.

Whatever may befall her, Ukraine will never forget the destruction and the losses she has suffered at the hands of Moscow.

---

*Pravda is the Russian word for "truth."

Index of Ukrainian Place Names

HARVARD UKRAINIAN RESEARCH INSTITUTE

Monograph Series

Ievhen Sverstiuk, *Clandestine Essays*, translated with an introduction by G.S.N. Luckyj. Littleton, Colo.: Ukrainian Academic Press, 1976.

Taras Hunczak (ed.), *The Ukraine, 1917–1921: A Study in Revolution*. Cambridge, Mass.: Harvard Ukrainian Research Institute, distributed by Harvard University Press, 1977.

Paul R. Magocsi, *The Shaping of a National Identity: Subcarpathian Rus', 1848– 1948*. Cambridge, Mass., and London: Harvard University Press, 1978.

Ivan Zilyns'kyj. *A Phonetic Description of the Ukrainian Language*, translated by W. T. Zyla and W. M. Aycock. Cambridge, Mass.: Harvard Ukrainian Research Institute, distributed by Harvard University Press, 1979.

George G. Grabowicz. *Toward a History of Ukrainian Literature*. Cambridge, Mass.: Harvard Ukrainian Research Institute, distributed by Harvard University Press, 1981.

Omeljan Pritsak, *The Origin of Rus'*, Vol. I. Cambridge, Mass.: Harvard Ukrainian Research Institute, distributed by Harvard University Press, 1981.

George G. Grabowicz, *The Poet as Mythmaker: A Study of Symbolic Meaning in Taras Ševčenko*. Cambridge, Mass.: Harvard Ukrainian Research Institute, distributed by Harvard University Press, 1982.

Andrei S. Markovits and Frank E. Sysyn (eds.), *Nationbuilding and the Politics of Nationalism: Essays on Austrian Galicia*. Cambridge, Mass.: Harvard Ukrainian Research Institute, distributed by Harvard University Press, 1982.

Paul R. Magocsi, *Galicia: An Historical Survey and Bibliographic Guide*. Toronto and Buffalo: University of Toronto Press, 1982.

Sources and Document Series

Proceedings of the Conference on Carpatho-Ruthenian Immigration, transcribed, edited and annotated by Richard Renoff and Stephen Reynolds. Cambridge, Mass.: Harvard Ukrainian Research Institute, 1975.

Nonconformity and Dissent in the Ukrainian SSR, 1955–1975: A Select Bibliography, compiled by George Liber and Anna Mostovych. Cambridge, Mass.: Harvard Ukrainian Research Institute, 1978.

The Cossack Administration of the Hetmanate, 2 vols., compiled by George Gajecky. Cambridge, Mass.: Harvard Ukrainian Research Institute, 1978.

An Early Slavonic Psalter from Rus': St. Catherine's Monastery, Mt. Sinai, Volume I: Photoreproduction, edited by Moshé Altbauer and Horace G. Lunt. Cambridge, Mass.: Harvard Ukrainian Research Institute, distributed by Harvard University Press, 1978.

The Ukrainian Experience in the United States: A Symposium, edited by Paul R. Magocsi. Cambridge, Mass.: Harvard Ukrainian Research Institute, 1979.

Occasional Papers

Omeljan Pritsak, *The Origin of Rus'* , Inaugural Lecture delivered at Harvard University, October 1975. Cambridge, Mass.: Harvard Ukrainian Research Institute, 1976.

HARVARD SERIES IN UKRAINIAN STUDIES

Eyewitness Chronicle (Litopys Samovydcja), Part I, edited by Orest Levyc'kyj. Munich: Fink Vlg., 1972.

George S. N. Luckyj. *Between Gogol' and Ševčenko*. Munich: Fink Vlg., 1971.

Myron Korduba, *La littérature historique soviétique ukrainienne*. Munich: Fink Vlg., 1972.

Oleksander Ohloblyn, *A History of Ukrainian Industry*. Munich: Fink Vlg., 1971.

Fedir Savčenko, *The Suppression of Ukrainian Activities in 1876* (Zaborona ukrajinstva 1876 r.). Munich: Fink Vlg., 1970.

The Galician-Volynian Chronicle, translated and annotated by George Perfecky, Munich: Fink Vlg., 1973.

Dmitrij Tschižewskij, *Skovoroda: Dichter, Denker, Mystiker*. Munich: Fink Vlg., 1974.